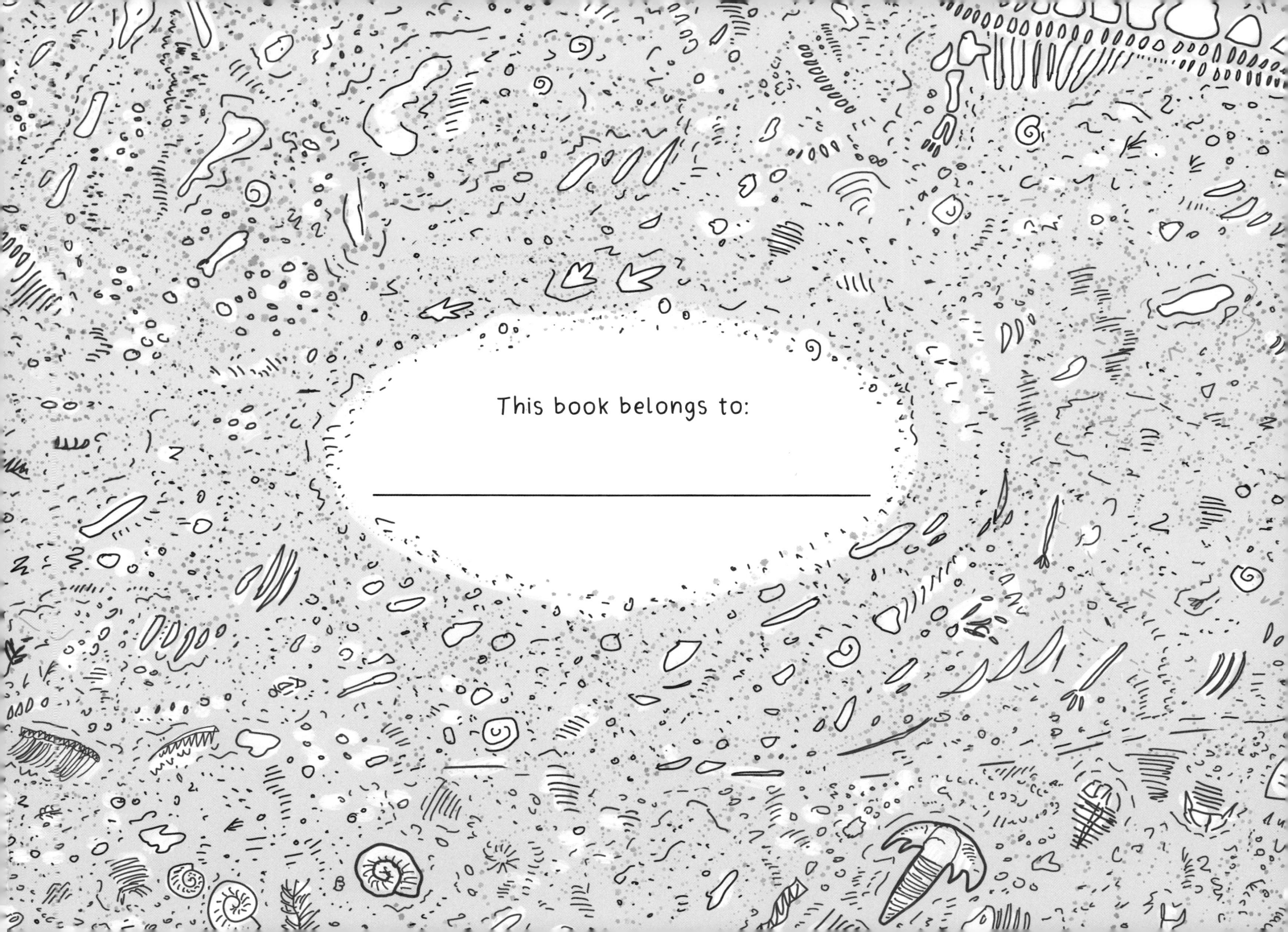

This book belongs to:

_____

FINDING ... A PREHISTORIC SEARCH & FIND LIFE

BY SOPHIE WILLIAMS

THE HISTORY OF
LIFE ON EARTH

Bacteria,
jellyfish and
sponges

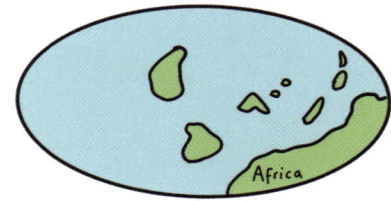

4,500
million
years ago

541
million years ago
(MYA)

485
MYA

443
MYA

419
MYA

359
MYA

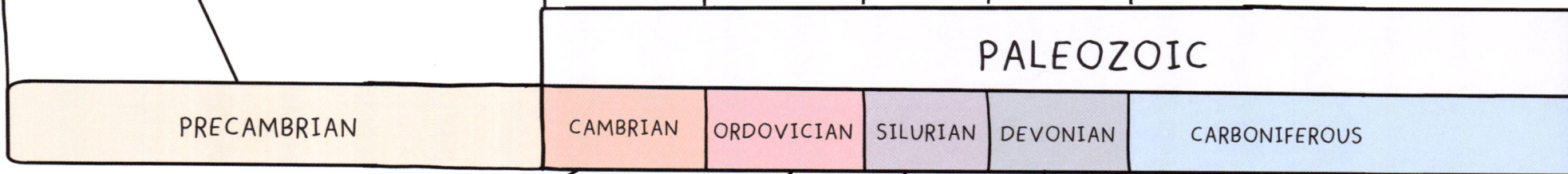

PALEOZOIC

PRECAMBRIAN

CAMBRIAN

ORDOVICIAN

SILURIAN

DEVONIAN

CARBONIFEROUS

Land plants

Amphibians, spiders,
flightless insects

Forests of trees,
flying insects

Fish

Cambrian Explosion:
molluscs, brachiopods, trilobites
and early vertebrates

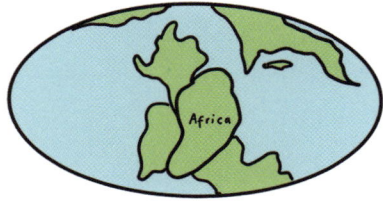  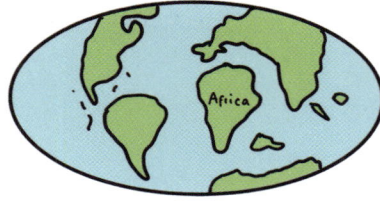

Humans
(300,000 years ago)

299
MYA

252
MYA

201
MYA

145
MYA

66
MYA

23
MYA

2.6
MYA

1.8
million
years ago

MESOZOIC

CENOZOIC

ERAS

PERMIAN | TRIASSIC | JURASSIC | CRETACEOUS | PALEOGENE | NEOGENE | QUARTERNARY

PERIODS

The
Ice Age

Birds

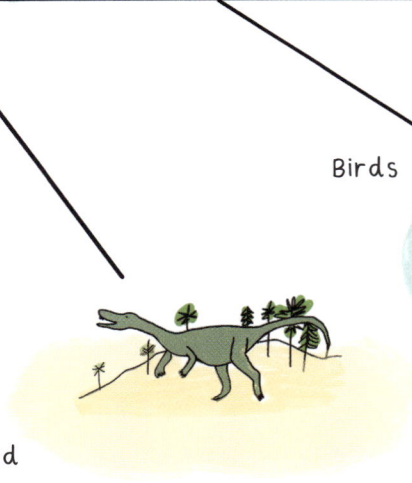

Dinosaurs and
small mammals

K-Pg extinction

THE BEGINNINGS OF LIFE
IN THE LATE PRECAMBRIAN

Our planet, Earth, formed about 4.5 billion years ago. At first, it was just a ball of molten rock spinning around the Sun. Slowly, over millions of years, the boiling planet cooled and a hard crust formed on its surface. A blanket of gases, called the atmosphere, surrounded the planet.

Many volcanoes exploded, spilling hot lava and filling the air with thick, toxic gas.

Meteors and comets often crashed into Earth, and scientists believe some of them brought ice. As Earth cooled, the planet filled with water. In those early oceans, simple, single-celled microorganisms appeared. These tiny, microscopic creatures could breathe and reproduce.

They were the very first lifeforms on Earth!

Around 3.5 billion years ago, some of the microorganisms learned to use sunlight to make their own food through photosynthesis. As they did this, they released oxygen as waste. Very gradually, the oxygen filled the atmosphere, making it possible for new life to evolve.

This special time is called the Precambrian era, and it lasted nearly three billion years... the longest period in Earth's history.

Some of the earliest animals were soft-bodied creatures, like simple jellyfish and sponges. Because they didn't have bones, there are almost no fossils of them, so we can only guess what they looked like. They were probably strange, blobby shapes! Over time, minerals washed into the seas, and lifeforms began to grow shells and skeletons, leaving behind fossils we can study today.

In the pages ahead, you'll hunt the landscapes for some truly amazing animals; from a giant scorpion to a tiny, turkey-sized dinosaur, and even a massive, Ice Age rhinoceros. But the strangest and most surprising creature of all is us humans! This is an incredible journey through time, and we're still discovering new parts of it today.

Enjoy the search, and don't forget to explore the glossary at the back to learn more about each fascinating beast!

THE CAMBRIAN PERIOD

541 → 485 MYA

About 541 million years ago, there was a huge burst of new life. Scientists call this the Cambrian Explosion. The oceans filled with shellfish called brachiopods. There were also arthropods, creatures with hard shells on the outside of their bodies. They were the ancestors of insects and crabs.

Another important group was the chordates, animals with a simple backbone. They were the ancestors of all animals with spines – including us, humans!

CAN YOU SPOT...

Wiwaxia →

Leanchoilia →

Lingula →

Pikaia →

Anomalocaris →

Odaraia →

THE ORDOVICIAN

485 → 443 MYA PERIOD

During the Ordovician period, new sea life emerged, including animals like snails, shellfish and coral. The first fish also appeared. These fish looked pretty strange. Instead of jaws, they had soft mouths that sucked up food like vacuums.

All the land was concentrated in one big, rocky supercontinent called Gondwana. Gradually, primitive plants began to grow on the land.

The weather started out very warm, but then it got much colder. Towards the end of the Ordovician, a huge extinction event caused 85% of all life on the planet to disappear.

CAN YOU SPOT...

Starfish →

Nautiloid →

Agnatha →

Conodont →

Arandaspis →

Lanarkia →

THE SILURIAN PERIOD

443 → 419 MYA

Life gradually returned after the Ordovician extinction. In the oceans, coral reefs started to form, providing a home for new sea creatures, including the first fish with jaws.

On land, mosses, simple plants and lichens (a mix of plants and fungi) began to grow. These plants slowly broke down the rocks and helped create soil. As time went on, more complex plants appeared, and so did flightless insects.

CAN YOU SPOT...

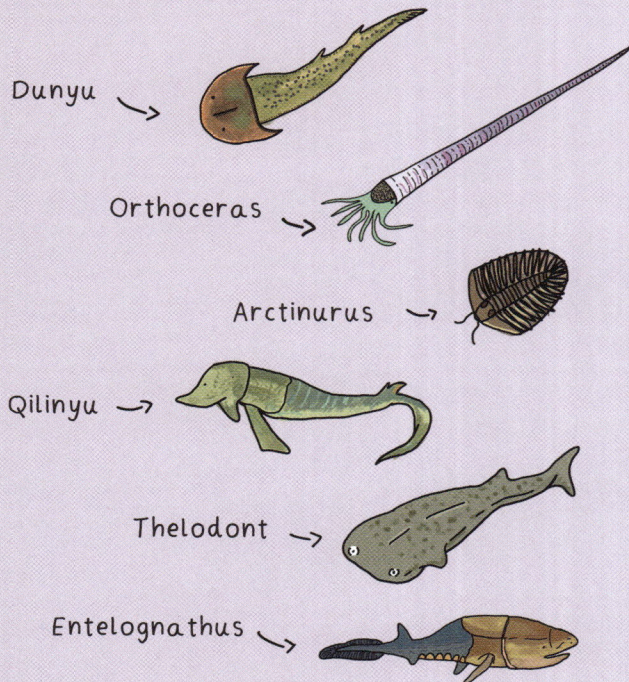

Dunyu →

Orthoceras →

Arctinurus →

Qilinyu →

Thelodont →

Entelognathus →

THE DEVONIAN

419 → 359 MYA PERIOD

The seas continued to fill with coral reefs and fish. Some fish developed powerful muscles inside their front fins. They were called lobe-finned fish.

On land, some plant species evolved to have seeds. As the plants developed, so did the insects. Soon, the fish in the seas began to emerge from the water to feed on the insects. The front fins of lobe-finned fish gradually evolved into limbs for walking on land. These creatures were called tetrapods, which means 'four feet' in Greek.

CAN YOU SPOT...

Parexus →

Dunkleosteus →

Onychodus →

Rhyniognatha →

Acanthostega →

Pterygotus →

THE CARBONIFEROUS PERIOD

359 → 299 MYA

In the Carboniferous, the climate was warm and tropical. The land was covered in forests of giant ferns and early trees. Many of the fossil fuels we use today, like coal and oil, come from the remains of plants and animals from this period.

During this time, tetrapods started to change. Some of them became amphibians, laying their soft, jelly-like eggs in water. Others developed a special kind of egg with a leathery shell that could survive on dry land. These animals were called amniotes. They were able to live away from the water, and over time, they evolved into reptiles and mammals.

CAN YOU SPOT...

Edaphosaurus

Pulmonoscorpius

Meganisoptera

Diplocaulus

Anthracodromeus

Onchiodon

THE PERMIAN

299 → 252 MYA   PERIOD

During the Permian, almost all of the land on Earth came together to form one huge supercontinent called Pangea. The middle of it became a giant, dry desert, and the rainforests of the Carboniferous gradually disappeared. New reptiles evolved to survive this harsh climate.

Near the end of the Permian, thousands of volcanoes erupted, filling the air with toxic gases and blocking the sun with ash clouds. 95% of ocean life and 70% of land animals died out in the biggest extinction event in Earth's history.

CAN YOU SPOT...

Dimetrodon

Inostrancevia

Cotylorhynchus

Tiarajudens

Procynosuchus

Diictodon

THE
TRIASSIC

252 → 201 MYA   PERIOD

After the great Permian Extinction, it took the Earth about 10 million years to recover. Slowly, life returned. New species of reptiles appeared, including the first dinosaurs. Without much competition, the dinosaurs adapted quickly to different environments.

The Earth's plates shifted, and Pangea began to break apart. More volcanic eruptions occurred, and at the end of the Triassic, there was another extinction event. Whilst many species were wiped out, the dinosaurs survived.

CAN YOU SPOT...

Ichthyosaurus

Aetosaurus

Eoraptor

Isanosaurus

Tanystropheus

Plesiosaurus

THE JURASSIC

201 → 145 MYA PERIOD

During the Jurassic, dinosaurs were kings! They evolved into all shapes and sizes. The climate was warm and wet, and huge plants covered the land, providing plenty of food for the herbivores, like Brachiosaurus. Fast, fierce hunters, like Allosaurus, preyed on the herbivores. Flying reptiles called pterosaurs filled the skies, and the first birds appeared.

Early mammals also evolved. They remained small, scurrying around on the forest floor, staying out of the way of the big, powerful dinosaurs.

CAN YOU SPOT...

Archaeopteryx →

Cryolophosaurus →

Guanlong →

Compsognathus →

Velociraptor →

Anurognathus →

THE
CRETACEOUS

145 → 66 MYA   PERIOD

In the Cretaceous, the continents drifted closer to where they are today. The very first flowers appeared, attracting new pollinators like beetles and flies.

Dinosaurs continued to rule. Tyrannosaurus rex was a giant carnivore, and Triceratops had horns and a bony frill. Duck-billed dinosaurs roamed in herds. In the skies, birds took the place of pterosaurs.

At the end of the period, a giant asteroid crashed into the planet. The impact caused a huge dust cloud which blocked out the Sun. Around 75% of life on Earth was wiped out, including all the dinosaurs. This is called the K-Pg extinction.

CAN YOU SPOT...

Deinosuchus
>

Parasaurolophus
>

Zuniceratops
>

Didelphodon
>

Confuciusornis
>

Hesperornis >

THE PALEOGENE

66 → 23 MYA   PERIOD

After the K-Pg extinction, the world was a different place. The dinosaurs were gone, and the mammals rose to take their place.

At the beginning of the period, the Earth was warm and covered in dense forests. The mammals stayed small. They looked like shrews, raccoons and tiny monkeys. Gradually, the climate cooled and big grasslands spread across the continents. With the open space, some mammals started to grow bigger and the ancestors of horses and whales evolved.

Birds also grew bigger, including huge, flightless birds the size of a bus, with razor-sharp talons.

CAN YOU SPOT...

Titanoboa →

Entolodon →

Smilodectes →

Miohippus →

Gastornis →

Mesonyx →

THE
NEOGENE
PERIOD
23 → 2.6 MYA

In the Neogene, the Earth looked a lot like it does today. The weather was cooler, and the big, open grasslands and savannahs kept spreading. New animals appeared, including the ancestors of giraffes, rhinos and elephants. Ancient cats and dogs evolved to chase after the grazing animals.

Monkeys grew bigger, and some evolved into large, tailless apes with big brains. Around seven million years ago, some apes began to walk on two feet. They were known as hominins.

CAN YOU SPOT...

Chalicotherium

Daphoenodon

Proailurus

Paraceratherium

Sivatherium

Australopithecus

THE PLEISTOCENE
EPOCH

2.6 MYA → 11,700 YEARS AGO

This period, often called the Ice Age, was a time when Earth's climate kept changing. Sometimes it was very cold, and giant glaciers covered the land. Other times, it warmed up, and the glaciers retreated. Mammals like mammoths and mastodons grew thick fur to withstand the cold.

Around 300,000 years ago, a hominin evolved with a very large brain. This hominin was called Homo Sapiens, or human. The humans did not have thick fur, but they were great communicators. This meant they could hunt in packs. Many of the large animals of the Pleistocene were hunted to extinction by humans.

CAN YOU SPOT...

Zygomaturus →

Aiolornis →

Murrayglossus →

kyptoceras →

Smilodon →

Glyptodon →

THE HOLOCENE

11,700 YEARS AGO → TODAY   EPOCH

The time we are living in today is called the Holocene. After the Ice Age, the Earth became warmer and many different ecosystems developed. Humans spread to new places. At first, they lived as hunter-gatherers, but then they settled down and began farming. Gradually, villages turned into towns turned into cities. The success of humans has come at a cost to the planet. Natural habitats have been destroyed to make space for settlements and farmland. Climate change has also made life hard for many plants and animals, and some have become extinct.

What will the future look like? The planet is always changing, and life will keep evolving in ways we can't even imagine! While we're here, it's our job to look after it and make sure it's a good home - not just for us, but for all the living things we share it with.

CAN YOU SPOT...

Gorilla →

Lemur

Dart Frog →
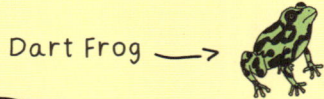

Tapir

Orangutan →

Hummingbird

THE FOSSIL RECORD

Scientists called paleontologists study fossils to find out how life on Earth has changed. Fossils are the traces of living things from the past. They form when a dead plant or animal gets buried under layers of mud, sand or ash. Over thousands of years, more layers build up, and the animal's body parts turn into stone.

Most fossils come from the hard parts of animals like bones, teeth, beaks and shells, because the soft parts usually rot away before they can become fossils. Like jigsaw pieces, paleontologists use these fragments to piece together what animals looked like, how they lived and how life on Earth has changed through time.

CAN YOU SPOT...

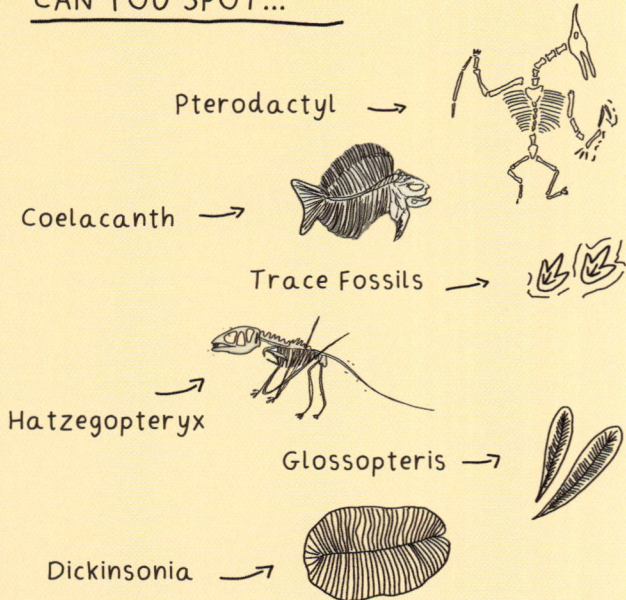

Pterodactyl →

Coelacanth →

Trace Fossils →

Hatzegopteryx →

Glossopteris →

Dickinsonia →

GLOSSARY

GENERAL TERMS

Amniotic egg → An egg with a hard shell that can withstand the dry land air. The evolution of the amniotic egg is what allowed fish to emerge fully onto land.

Arthropod → Animals with hard shells and lots of legs, like bugs, crabs and spiders.

Brachiopod → Sea animals with two shells, like clams.

Carnivore → An animal that only eats meat.

Chordate → Animals with a backbone, or something like a backbone, inside their body. All vertebrates are chordates.

Coprolites → Fossilised animal poo that can tell us what animals ate and how they lived.

Cyanobacteria → Tiny, ancient bacteria that used sunlight to make food and helped fill the atmosphere with oxygen.

Cynodont → The ancient ancestors of mammals. They usually had fur.

Herbivore → An animal that only eats plants.

Hominin → Great apes that walked on two legs. Humans are the only surviving species of hominin.

Invertebrate → An animal that doesn't have a backbone, like insects, worms or jellyfish.

Mammal → An animal that has hair or fur, gives birth to live young and feeds its babies with milk produced in its body.

Paleontology → The science of studying fossils to learn about life long ago.

Sauropod → Big, long-necked dinosaurs that ate plants and walked on four legs.

Sedimentary rock → A type of rock made from layers of mud, sand, or small pieces of other rocks. This is where fossils can be found.

Theropod → Dinosaurs that walked on two legs and mostly ate meat, like Allosaurus or Tyrannosaurus rex.

Trace fossil → A fossil that shows signs of an animal's activity, like footprints or burrows.

Vertebrate → Animals that have spines, like fish, birds and people.

CAMBRIAN

Wiwaxia → A soft-bodied animal covered in scales and spines to protect it from predators.

Leanchoilia → A marine arthropod with long claws and four eyes.

Lingula → A brachiopod, or shellfish, that is still around today.

Pikaia → A flat, eel-like creature with an early backbone called a notochord.

Anomalocaris → A prawn-like arthropod that ate worms and plankton.

Odaraia → A tube-shaped arthropod predator.

ORDOVICIAN

Starfish → A five-armed starfish that looked a lot like starfish today.

Nautiloid → A shellfish with a coiled shell. Only its head and tentacles were exposed to the outside world.

Agnatha → An eel-like jawless fish that was the earliest vertebrate that we know of.

Conodont → A jawless fish that had cone-shaped tooth-like structures in its mouth.

Arandaspis → A small, jawless fish with a paddle-like tail and raindrop-shaped scales.

Lanarkia → A jawless fish covered in small, spiny scales.

SILURIAN

Dunyu → An armoured, jawless fish known for its bony head shield.

Orthoceras → A horn-shaped nautiloid shellfish.

Arctinurus → A large trilobite with spines and a broad body.

Qilinyu → A fish that was one of the first to have the beginnings of a jawbone and lobe fins.

Thelodont → A small, jawless fish with unusual scale patterns.

Entelognathus → One of the first properly jawed fishes.

DEVONIAN

Parexus → A spiny, shark-like fish with a long, pointy dorsal fin on its back.

Dunkleosteus → A big armoured fish with powerful jaws and bony plates.

Onychodus → A huge lobe-finned fish with a retractable tusk that it could thrust out in times of attack.

Rhyniognatha → The earliest insect ever discovered. It had big jaws for eating leaves.

Acanthostega → One of the earliest tetrapods. It had limbs and toes, but it couldn't walk on land – it used its limbs for paddling and grabbing onto aquatic plants.

Pterygotus → A carnivorous marine arthropod reaching up to 1.8 m (6 ft) long.

CARBONIFEROUS

Edaphosaurus → One of the earliest-known, large, plant-eating land animals. It had a sail on its back to cool its body down.

Pulmonoscorpius → A giant, cat-sized scorpion

Meganisoptera → A huge dragonfly-type insect with a wingspan of 70 cm (2.3 ft).

Diplocaulus → A big, dog-sized tetrapod with a boomerang-shaped head.

Anthracodromeus → A small tetrapod with a long body and small limbs.

Onchiodon → A small salamander-like amphibian.

PERMIAN

Dimetrodon → Often mistaken for a dinosaur, Dimetrodon lived 40 million years before the dinosaurs. It was a large predator with a sail on its back.

Inostrancevia → A sabre-toothed predator that was about the size of a tiger with skin like an elephant. It was an ancestor of mammals.

Cotylorhynchus → This strange-looking herbivore had a very big body, very small legs and a tiny head. It was the size of a bus.

Tiarajudens → A sabre-toothed herbivore about the size of a wild boar.

Procynosuchus → One of the earliest cynodonts (mammal ancestors). It was 6 cm (2.3 in) long and spent most of its time in water, paddling with its wide feet and rudder-like tail.

Diictodon → A cynodont with a large head and a horny beak. It spent most of its time in burrows, where it could escape the desert heat.

TRIASSIC

Icthyosaurus → A large, fast-swimming marine reptile that looked a bit like a dolphin.

Aetosaurus → A close relation of crocodiles. It had a small head, an upturned snout and rows of plate armour.

Eoraptor → One of the earliest-known dinosaurs. It measured around 1 m (3.2 ft) long with long back legs and sharp teeth for eating amphibians and small reptiles.

Isanosaurus → One of the oldest known sauropods that walked properly on four legs.

Tanystropheus → A marine reptile with a neck that was longer than its body and tail combined.

Plesiosaurus → A large marine reptile with a small head, long neck and flippers.

CRETACEOUS

Deinosuchus → A giant relative of alligators, reaching 10 m (33 ft) long.

Parasaurolophus → A duck-billed dinosaur with a long, curved head crest.

Zuniceratops → This dinosaur looked like Triceratops, with a similar frilled crown and horns, but was much smaller, reaching only 3 m (9.8 ft) long.

Didelphodon → An early relative of the North American opossum. It was the size of a small dog and lived in burrows.

Confuciusornis → One of the first proper beaked, toothless birds. It was the size of a crow.

Hesperornis → A large, 2 m (6.5 ft) long, flightless bird that looked a bit like a cormorant. It swam in the oceans and snared fish with a tooth-lined beak.

JURASSIC

Archaeopteryx → A feathered dinosaur-bird hybrid. It had teeth and a tail like the velociraptor it evolved from, but it had wings and a beak like modern birds.

Cryolophosaurus → Early theropod with a distinctive crest on its head.

Guanlong → A small theropod, reaching 3 m (10 ft) long, which was an ancestor of Tyrannosaurus. It had three long fingers on its hands and a large crest on its head.

Compsognathus → A small, carnivorous theropod dinosaur around the size of a chicken.

Velociraptor → A small, feathered, carnivorous dinosaur. It had muscular legs, sharp claws and a long, stiff tail that helped it steer when running at high speeds.

Anurognathus → An early, insect-eating pterosaur with a wide head and big eyes.

PALEOGENE

Titanoboa → A giant, semi-aquatic snake that grew up to 14 m (46 ft) long and ate fish. It was one of the largest reptiles to evolve after the K-Pg extinction event.

Entolodon → A boar-like mammal with a big body, a long snout and skinny legs.

Smilodectes → A small primate with big eyes that lived in the tree canopy and ate leaves.

Miohippus → A small early horse with long legs and three toes on each foot.

Gastornis → A huge, flightless bird that reached around 2 m (6.5 ft), with a large head, sharp talons and a giant beak.

Mesonyx → A wolf-like predator with a large head and a long neck.

NEOGENE

Chalicotherium → This ancestor of horses and rhinos had long curved claws, rather than hooves. It knuckle-walked like a gorilla.

Daphoenodon → A carnivore that looked like a giant dog but with a long, flexible, cat-like body that was built for chasing prey on the open plains.

Proailurus → The ancestor of the entire cat family. It was the size of a house-cat, but looked more like a mongoose, with a long body, a pointy face and big eyes.

Paraceratherium → A giant, long-necked, hornless rhinoceros that at 7.4 m (24.3 ft) long is one of the largest land mammals to have ever existed.

Sivatherium → An ancestor of the giraffe that looked like a large okapi with moose-like horns.

Australopithecus → A small-bodied and small-brained early hominin. It walked on two feet but had ape-like features. It probably spent a lot of time in trees.

PLEISTOCENE

Zygomturus → A huge wombat-like marsupial that spent most of its time in swampy water.

Aiolornis → A giant condor-like bird with a wingspan of 5 m (16 ft) and a massive beak. It was the largest known bird capable of flight.

Murrayglossus → A huge echidna.

Kyptoceras → A small antelope-like animal with two small nose horns and two horns above its eyes that curved over its head.

Smilodon → Known as a sabre-toothed tiger, this predator was not actually related to the cat family.

Glyptodon → A giant armadillo.

HOLOCENE

Gorilla → Big apes that live in forests and are endangered because of habitat loss.

Lemur → Small, tree-dwelling animals with big eyes from Madagascar.

Dart Frog → Tiny, colourful frogs that can be poisonous.

Tapir → Big animals with short trunks, like a mix between a pig and an elephant.

Orangutan → Large, orange apes that live in trees and are critically endangered because of forest loss.

Hummingbird → Tiny birds that flap their wings super fast and drink flower nectar. They are becoming rarer.

FOSSIL RECORD

Pterodactyl → A large flying reptile (pterosaur) with a long beak that lived at the time of the dinosaurs.

Coelacanth → A rare, ancient fish thought to be extinct, but found alive in the ocean in 1938.

Trace Fossils → Marks or tracks left by animals long ago, like footprints or burrows.

Hatzegopteryx → A pterosaur with a giant head and short neck.

Glossopteris → An ancient plant with tongue-shaped leaves that helped scientists learn about the movement of Earth's continents.

Dickinsonia → One of the oldest known animals that lived in the sea. It was boneless and looked like an oval, ribbed pancake.

Other books you might like

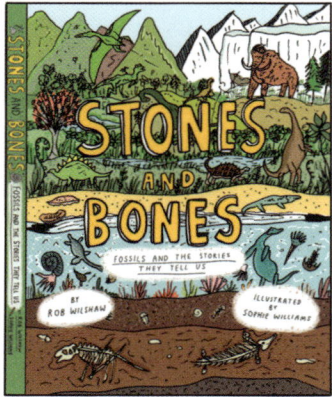

Stones and Bones: Fossils and the Stories They Tell
Rob Wilshaw and Sophie Williams

9781800660427 / Hardcover / 230 x 295mm / 80pp / £16.99 / $21.99

This book looks at the fossil record and all that we can learn from it. From bacteria to sponges to fish to tetrapods to reptiles to dinosaurs to mammals and finally to humans, it excavates the story of four billion years of life on this planet and brings it to life in lively, vivid illustrations.

A Books For Topics Recommended Read for Year 5, 2025-2026.
Shortlisted for the UKLA Book Awards 2025.

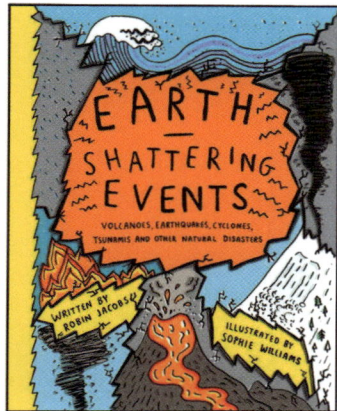

Earth Shattering Events: Volcanoes, Earthquakes, Cyclones, Tsunamis and Other Natural Disasters
Robin Jacobs and Sophie Williams

9781908714701 / Hardcover / 230 x 290 mm / 96pp / £16.99 / $22.99

We humans take our domination of the planet for granted, but sometimes the Earth reminds us that this is an illusion. This book explores nature at its most dramatic... and its most destructive. With clear, engaging explanations and dynamic illustrations, it captures the intensity and power of these natural phenomena.

An eye-opening and -widening introduction to our restless planet.
Kirkus Starred Review

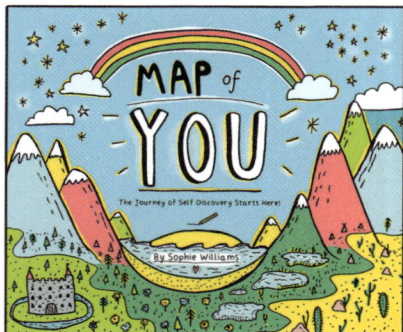

Map of You: The Journey of Self-Discovery Starts Here!
Sophie Williams

9781800660151 / Paperback / 210 x 270mm / 72 pp / £9.99 / $12.99

This charming activity book encourages young readers to to navigate the landscape of their own psyche by colouring, writing, doodling, drawing and completing personality quizzes. A fun and empowering way to help young people engage with mental well-being.

About the Author/Illustrator

Sophie Williams is a Cornish author and illustrator. Her bright, informative style of drawing is inspired by illustrators such as Nick Sharratt and Gemma Correll and from the landscapes that surround her in Cornwall. She is the illustrator of *Earth Shattering Events* (Cicada, 2019), *Stones and Bones* (Cicada, 2023) and the author of *Map of You* (Cicada, 2021).

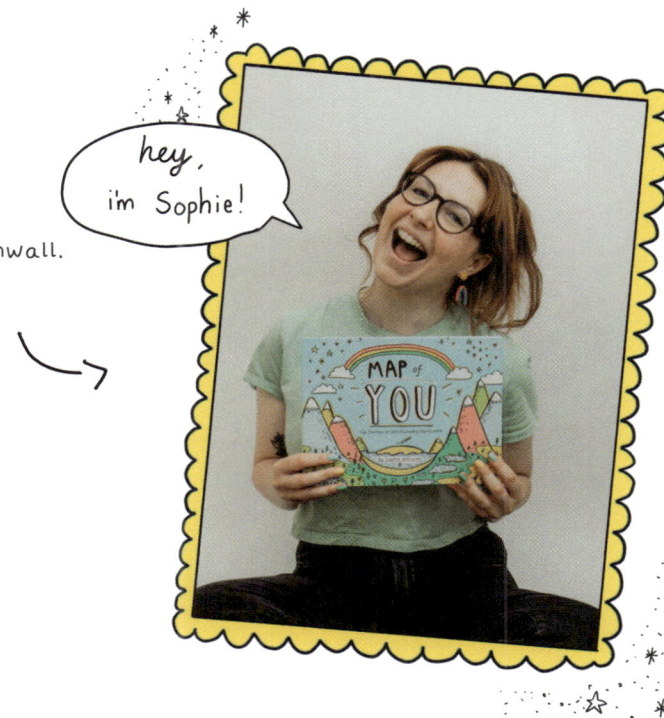

hey, i'm Sophie!

FINDING LIFE

Text by Sophie Williams, Ziggy Hanaor and Rob Wilshaw
Illustrations by Sophie Williams

British Library Cataloguing-in-Publication Data.

A CIP record for this book is available from the British Library
ISBN: 978-1-80066-054-0

First published in the UK in 2025, in the US in 2026.

Cicada Books Ltd
48 Burghley Road
London, NW5 1UE
www.cicadabooks.co.uk

© Cicada Books Ltd, 2025

Printed in Poland on FSC certified paper